The Cartoons
of
Douglas Harding

The Cartoons
of
Douglas Harding

THE SHOLLOND TRUST

The Cartoons of Douglas Harding

Published by The Shollond Trust
UK Charity Nº 1059551

© The Shollond Trust 2020

Cover design: rangsgraphics.com

Interior design: Richard Lang

All rights reserved.

The Shollond Trust, 87B Cazenove Road, London N16 6BB.
www.headless.org

ISBN: 978-1-908774-75-0

Preface

In 1937 Douglas Harding moved from England to India with his wife, Beryl, to join an architectural firm in Calcutta. He was 28 and had by then been working as an architect for about five years. He had also written a collection of short stories, *The Crimson Tiger*, and his first book, *The Meaning and Beauty of the Artificial*. Soon after arriving in India he became a father — Julian was born in 1937, Simon in 1938.

Though he was now managing a large architectural team, Harding continued thinking, reading and writing about what was closest to his heart, the subject of 'who he really was'. In 1941 he completed another book, *An Unconventional Portrait of Yourself*. But though the subject of his 'true identity' was his primary focus, Harding found time to write a detective novel (published in London in 1940), give talks on the radio, write articles about architecture, and assemble a portfolio of photographs of people, street scenes, buildings, and views of the Himalayas. (He was awarded a 'certificate of merit' for a photograph that was then displayed in the Indian Museum in Calcutta.) Harding wasn't twiddling his thumbs when he wasn't designing buildings.

Harding also became a well-respected cartoonist. In 1941 he held an exhibition of his cartoons in Calcutta, and his cartoons appeared in the press. In fact he was invited to become the principal cartoonist for the principal daily paper in India, *The Statesman* — his work was highly regarded. But by then Harding was a Major in the Army and his Brigadier forbade him to take up the invitation, saying it was not appropriate for an officer.

As a cartoonist Harding developed a high technical standard, and his own somewhat macabre style — a style of drawing that never really left him throughout the rest of his life. You can recognise it in his illustrations for his novel *The Spectre in the Lake*, written in the early 1990s. Late in his life Harding commented that he thought his early cartoon drawings had merit but the jokes were weak. Generally the jokes are dated, but they are amusing and show that Harding had a sense of humour. His cartoons also reflect the rather peculiar world of the British in India in the decade before the Second World War — the world of Empire and privilege, of snobbishness, chauvinism and racism. Harding had a perceptive eye and his cartoons are a critique of the society around him.

Harding saw who he really was in 1943. Immediately understanding he had discovered something of immense value, it was not long before he realised he had a great deal of work ahead of him if he was going to make sense of his discovery in terms of modern science. Deciding to focus his energies fully on this project, he gave up writing detective novels, taking photographs and drawing cartoons. The book that eventually emerged was *The Hierarchy of Heaven and Earth*. It was published in 1952 with an introduction by C.S. Lewis.

Nevertheless, Harding kept his cartoons. They had a place in his heart. (The copies we have are all larger than the size reproduced in this book, and all are on stiff card.) Incidentally, the cartoon on page 50 looks as though he used the space around the original cartoon for experimenting with other ideas. Many of these small drawings on this page are similar to illustrations in his book, *An Unconventional Portrait of Yourself*, so probably they were drawn in or before 1941. (All the cartoons reproduced here in this book were drawn between 1937 and 1943.)

We are publishing this collection of Harding's cartoons because we like them. But also because it gives insight into the creative life and character of a man who was a talented artist as well as what he later became — a great writer, philosopher and spiritual teacher.

Richard Lang

Cartoons

"Gee, Mr. Jones, do you still believe
that stork stuff? Listen, what really happens is..."

"It seems rather a shame to convert her."

"He has thirteen wives,
and Lord knows how many porcupines."

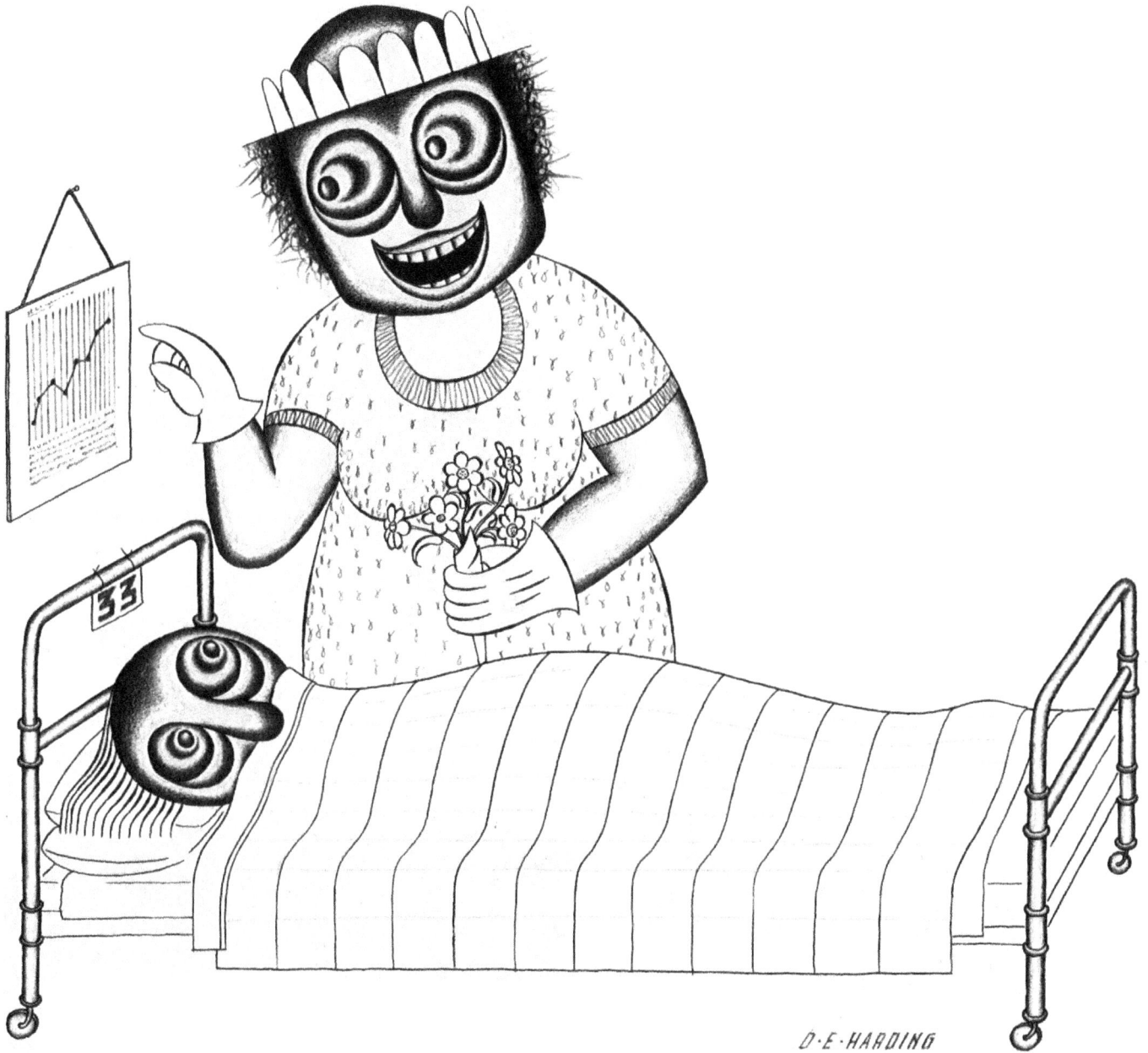

"Angina! My, what a pretty name!"

"But you must *try* not to be jealous of them, darling."

"My dear, she calls table napkins
serviettes — need I say more?"

"He says he's fallen in love at first sight."

"But I told you to send foundation *garments*."

"The fat one believes in storks and the thin one in gooseberry bushes — but why disillusion them?"

"What guarantee have I they're not really tapeworm's eggs?"

"Incidentally, Matilda, do tapeworms lay eggs?"

"I think he's just got worms."

"And how long, may I ask,
do you expect our permanent waves to last?"

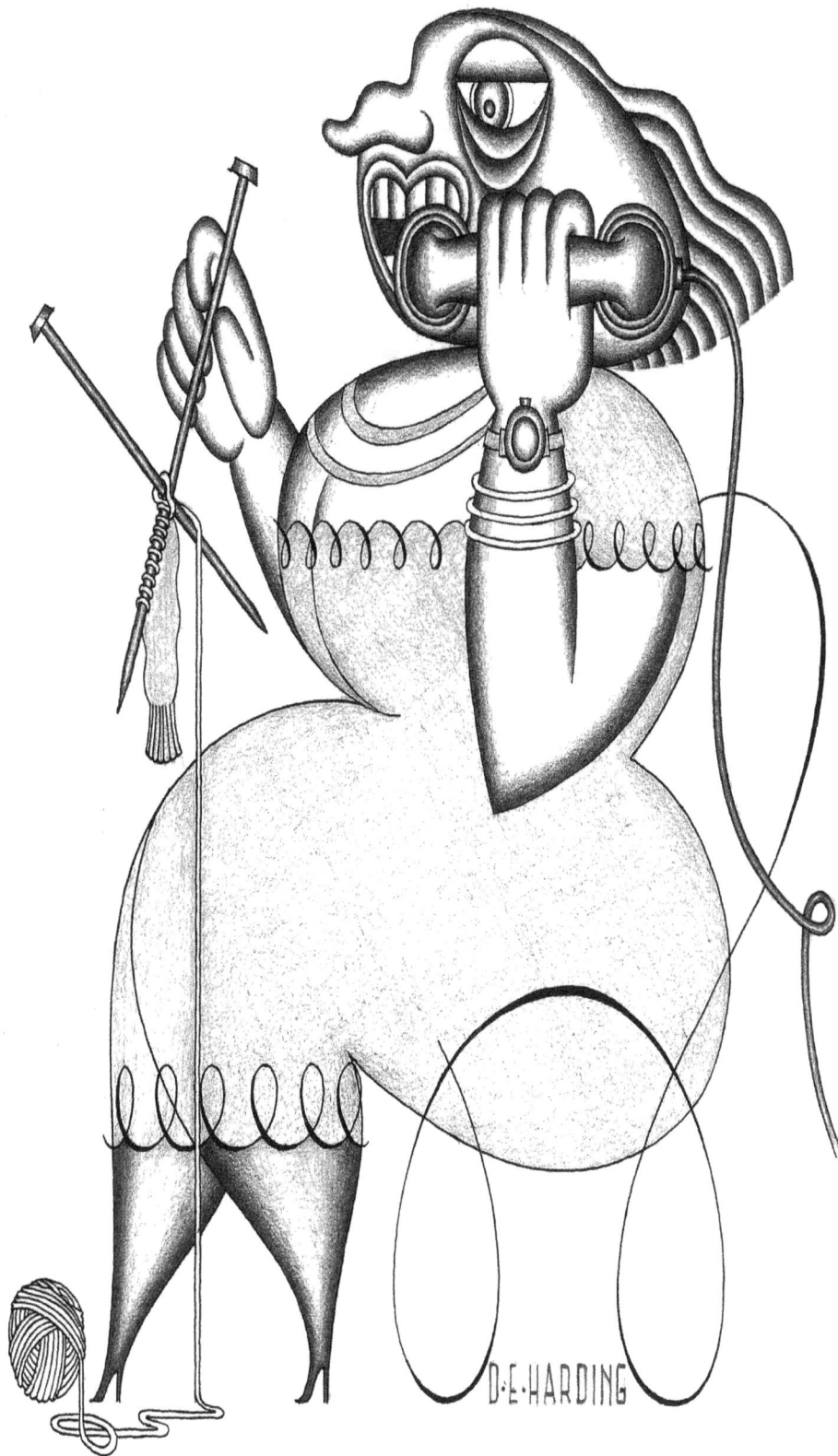

"But I must know *exactly* how big the Fleet Air Arm
is — never mind why."

"But I must know *exactly* how big the Fleet Air Arm
is — never mind why."

"You see, darling, Daddy is really a kind of stamen."

"I'm simply a harmless lunatic who wants
an electric fitting that looks like an electric fitting."

"Do you *still* think it's perfectly good soup?"

18

"Do you *still* think it's perfectly good soup?"

19

"Do you *still* think it's perfectly good soup?"

"Innocence my foot!
They're absolutely *riddled* with sex."

"Stool-pigeon."

"He insists we make an honest father-in-law of him."

CAKES
AS MOTHER
MAKES THEM

- D E HARDING -

"Surely we're not going to that shop, Mummie."

"Surely they're not *all* that bad."

- D·E·HARDING -

"But it was you who told me
to keep it under lock and key."

"He says may he have next Friday off
to take part in the communal riots."

"But my dear, tulips *date* so."

-D·E·HARDING-

30

"I can't make up my mind whether
my bathroom shall be Tudor or Jacobean."

-D·E·HARDING-

BLAZO
THE *DISTINCTIVE*
PERSONAL
METAL
POLISH

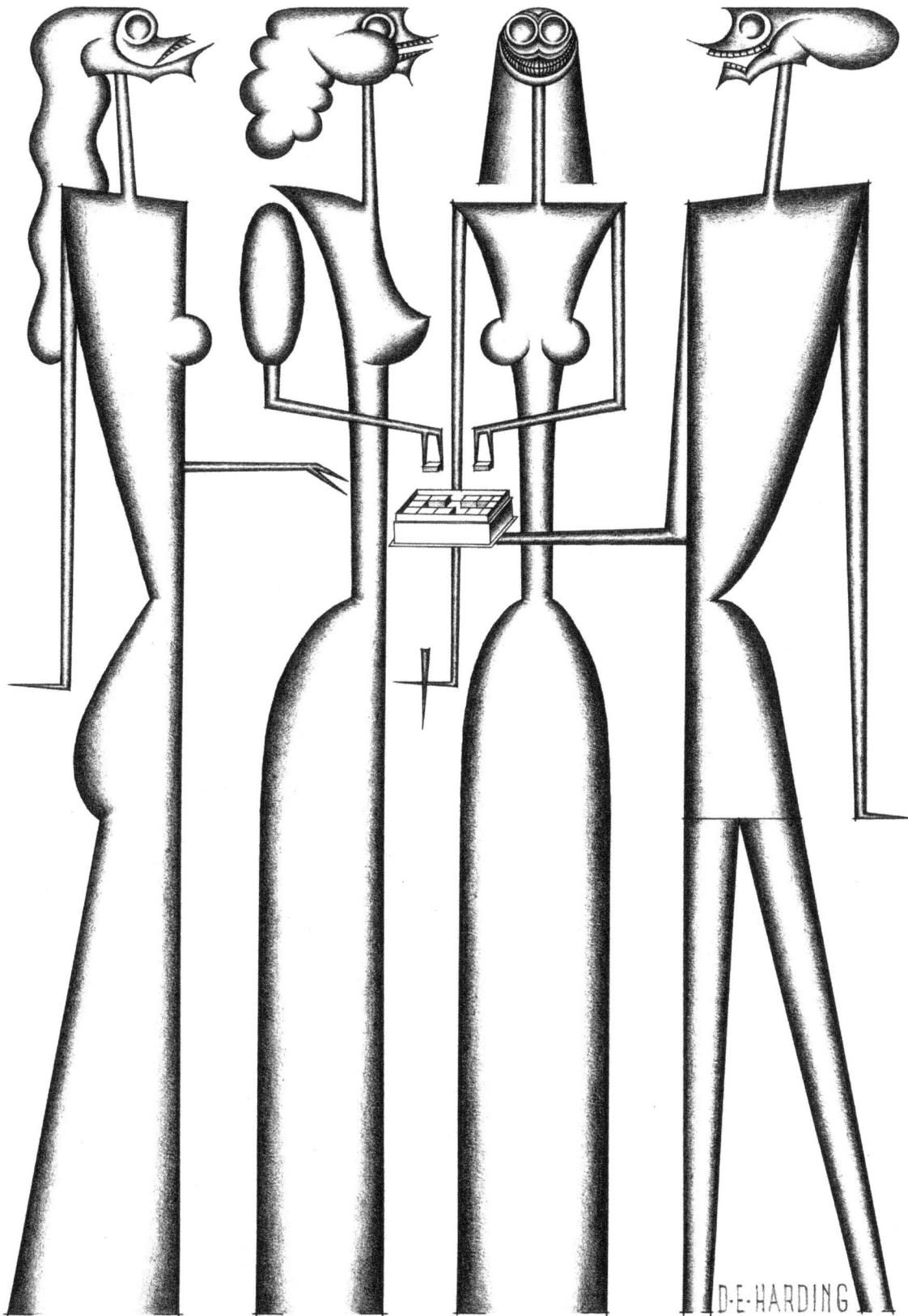

"They all have hard centres."

"She's bought the copyright
from her chauffeur, the ex-duke."

"And where does madam wear her mouth?"

"Bassinet."

D·E·HARDING

- D·E·HARDING -

"As a topic of conversation, dearie, your spotless
maidenhood is beginning to bore me."

D·E·HARDING

"Isn't Nature wonderful!"

"Something seems to interfere with my backhand drive."

"Look how human he acts, and he used to be *so* beastly."

"She used to be a woman of easy virtue,
but now she finds it more difficult."

D · E · HARDING

"All the same, Miss Fortescue,
I doubt whether the court will make them *all* pay."

"All the same, Miss Fortescue,
I hardly think the court will make them *all* pay."

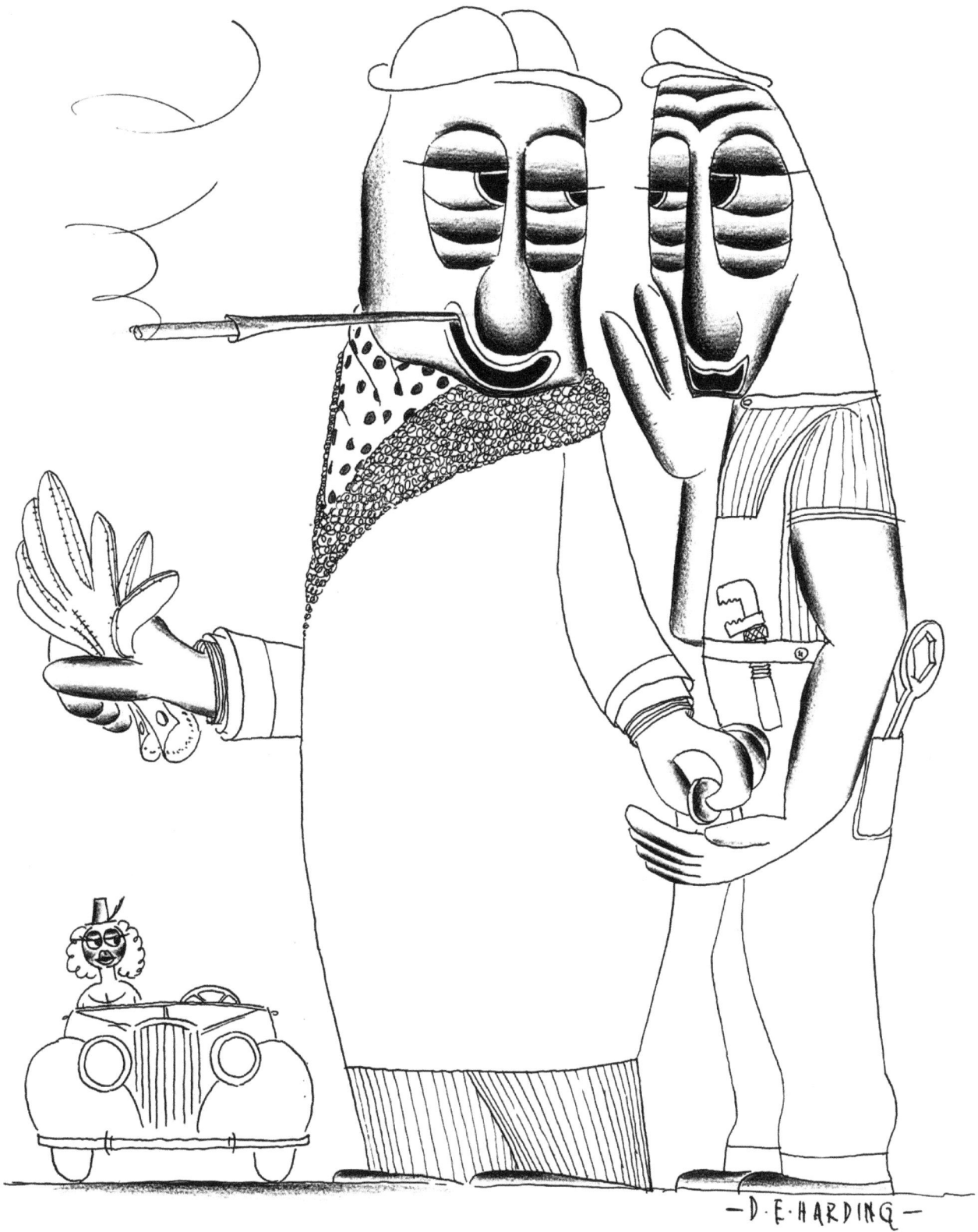

"Breakdown guaranteed."

"My God! They've emptied the pool!"

"Keeping abreast of the times — not getting
behind — Oh dear, it's all *so* difficult."

"Anyway I've stopped it gaining."

"Anyway I've stopped it gaining."

"Anyway I've stopped it gaining."

"If I'm rude, so's he."

"Every day at 3.15 she contacts the Cosmos."